⊞ ... OUR WONDERMENT INCREASES AS WE SEE THE LIVING ROOM.... HOW BROAD IT IS — AND QUIET.... THE BROAD SUNLIT WINDOWS, THE DIVANS UNDERNEATH, WITH BROAD RESTFUL BACKS AND SEATS. THE FIREPLACE? THE HEART OF THE WHOLE AND OF THE BUILDING ITSELF. ⊞

— FRANK LLOYD WRIGHT

"ARCHITECT, ARCHITECTURE, AND THE CLIENT," 1896

FRANK LLOYD WRIGHT'S
FIREPLACES

⊞   C A R L A   L I N D   ⊞

AN ARCHETYPE PRESS BOOK
POMEGRANATE ARTBOOKS, SAN FRANCISCO

Library of Congress Cataloging-in-Publication Data

Lind, Carla.

Frank Lloyd Wright's fireplaces / Carla Lind.

    p.   cm.   — (Wright at a glance)

"An Archetype Press book."

Includes bibliographical references.

ISBN 0-87654-469-3

1. Wright, Frank Lloyd, 1867–1959 — Criticism and interpretation. 2. Fireplaces. I. Title. II. Series: Lind, Carla. Wright at a glance.

NA3050.L56 1995   95-419

728'.37'092—dc20   CIP

Published by

Pomegranate Artbooks

Box 6099, Rohnert Park,

California 94927-6099

Catalogue no. A797

Produced by Archetype Press, Inc.

Washington, D.C.

Project Director: Diane Maddex

Editorial Assistants:

Gretchen Smith Mui, Kristi Flis,

and Christina Hamme

Designer: Robert L. Wiser

10 9 8 7 6 5 4 3 2

Printed in Singapore

Opening photographs: Page 1: Frank Lloyd Wright in his studio at Taliesin West, 1947. Page 2: The fireplace inglenook at Wright's Home and Studio in Oak Park. Pages 6–7: A ket-tle warming in the Taliesin fireplace.

CONTENTS

NTEGRITY IS THE BEGINNING AND THE END of every building designed by Frank Lloyd Wright (1867–1959). The interrelationship of each element, together with the harmony and the power of the total composition, defines the greatness of his work. But it is equally interesting to focus on individual features, such as his fireplaces. Whether we look only at a fireplace in a room or at the hearth as one part of a unique design, his versatility and genius are confirmed.

Wright designed more than one thousand fireplaces; no two are alike. The one consistent feature of all his houses was the presence—the dominant presence—of a fireplace, the heart of the home. It is a design and structural element worthy of celebration.

When our ancestors first gathered together, they did so around a fire. It was the focus of their assembly. In fact, *focus* is Latin for fireplace. At a fireside, our primordial memory is aroused; we feel secure and bonded to others. Even after furnaces and stoves provided sufficient heat for our houses, the fireplace retained its symbolic position as a sign of comfort and protection.

After eight decades of change, the living room fireplace at Wright's Wisconsin home, Taliesin (1911–59), has become less rustic, more refined in form. Its rough limestone was used throughout the rambling house.

· 9

The large stone hearth at Taliesin became a stage for formal and informal musicial events. Wright learned from his father how to play the piano, and he took every opportunity when he was there.

One mantel manufacturer at the turn of the century acknowledged the depth of those feelings in its advertisements. "The thought a fireplace creates is first of all ancestral. It means you have a father and a home." The ad continued to tap the powerful symbolism, concluding that a fireplace is "a symbol of three virtues: illumination, warmth and purification.... A place for fire is also an altar; that is an altar for sacrifice, for refuge, for love."

The critic John Ruskin tied domestic architecture to domestic virtues when he wrote in the mid-nineteenth century about the relationship of beauty, architecture, and morality. Ruskin declared that every house should have prominent chimneys and fireplaces to help evoke the values of trust, protection, and traditional bonds. Other proponents of the Arts and Crafts style agreed. A fireplace meant that the family was important at home and that it was stable. Every house, even the smallest cottage, should have a fireplace. The larger the house, the larger the fireplace and usually the mantel.

Fireplaces were the focal points of Wright's living spaces. He designed a total of forty-four for his own

three homes—nearly one per room—so that he could be constantly surrounded by their glow. Each of his fireplaces was masterful in its proportion and use of materials. Creating a fireplace was an opportunity for Wright to combine his skill at handling planes and masses with that of the material, the third dimension. His hearths were usually built of brick or stone, but at times he incorporated wood, tile, or glass. Generally symmetrical in the early years and asymmetrical later on, Wright's fireplaces mark his shift in orientation from the formality of the Victorian era to the informality of the industrial age.

No matter how he simplified his residential designs through the seventy years of his career, Wright retained a massive fireplace as a central element, both architecturally and spiritually. In the 1930s, when he reassessed the design of the American house, eliminating all that was unnecessary, he kept the hearth despite the fact that it was essential for neither cooking nor heating. Wright never suggested removing the fireplace as a means to cut costs. To do so would have cut the soul out of a building.

⊞ The hearth should be the place about which people gather; but the mantelpiece in the average American house, being ugly, is usually covered with inflammable draperies; the fire is, in consequence, rarely lit, and no one cares to sit about a fireless hearth. ⊞

Edith Wharton and
Ogden Codman
The Decoration of Houses, 1897

At the Hollyhock house (1917), Hollywood, a geometric abstraction carved into the mantelpiece is believed to represent "The Princess and the Desert" and includes a stylized hollyhock motif like others created for the house.

FIREPLACE DESIGN

⠿ Each material has its own message and, to the creative artist, its own song. It is easier to use them solo or in duet than manifold. ⠿

Frank Lloyd Wright

"In the Cause of Architecture,"

Architectural Record, 1928

The hexagonal module of the Hanna house (1936), Palo Alto, California, called for unusual masonry forms. For this early Usonian residence, Wright chose red brick and integrated the ornament with corner corbeling, terminating in a hexagonal hearth.

WRIGHT TENDED TO MOLD A FIRE-place out of an entire wall rather than cut a hole and apply a frame to it. This sculptural approach and his delight in the materials used contributed to the visual power of his designs.

The majority of Wright's fireplaces were constructed of brick, which by the 1890s was available in a wide variety of finishes, shapes, and textures in countless shades of yellow, red, and brown. For Wright, brick did not have to be restricted to the exterior of a building but could be used for interior wall surfaces, unplastered. The machine-given, right-angled quality of brick was ideally suited to his rectilinear designs. Roman brick, longer and narrower than standard brick, reiterated the horizontal lines that Wright favored. To further accentuate the horizontality, he usually specified deeply raked horizontal mortar joints in a contrasting color and vertical joints that were tinted to match the brick and cut flush with the face.

In 1928 Wright wrote a moving essay on stone, his beloved building material. He liked to see it stacked in stratified layers just as it forms naturally. To achieve this,

he tightly set rugged limestone blocks—with their rustic surfaces, random sizes, and irregular projections—on shallow mortar beds. He used limestone, sandstone, field stone, granite, and even desert ruble stone—whatever was native—so that a building would become a natural extension of the surrounding earth.

The aesthetics of these sculptural compositions sometimes superseded their functional requirements. Contrary to conventional thinking on the proper dimensions for a good-drawing fireplace, Wright preferred wide openings and low chimneys. Unlike today's fireplaces, dampers, flue liners, ash dumps, and screens were rarely specified, and Wright ignored the recommended one-to-eight relationship of flue to fireplace opening. If clients complained about a poor draft, he would advise them to build a bigger fire or raise the fire in a grate.

Wright decried multiple chimney spires projecting from housetops as "sooty fingers that threatened the sky." He pulled together all the chimneys into one broad, low form in proportion to the house. As with all other functional elements, they became integral to the design.

Anchors of the house

Part of the central masonry mass, creating a pivotal architectural point for the structure

Cavelike centers

A deep, beckoning space, contrasting with the open floor plan

Large openings

An oversized opening that helps define the entire wall

Natural materials

Predominantly local stone, various types of brick (especially roman brick), tile, and concrete

Integrated design

Expression of the grammar and materials of the house, repeating motifs used elsewhere

Perfect scale

Proportions scaled for the particular space

Massive bases

Large plinth blocks, with stone shoulders at the base of the opening

Prominent lintels

Exaggerated cross pieces, usually of stone or cast concrete

Few mantelpieces

Simple planes instead of traditional decorative shelves

Integral ornament

Artistic manipulation of materials to create rather than apply ornament

Custom hardware

Specially designed fixtures such as andirons. No screens

Intimate gatherings

Built-in seating to draw family and guests near the fire

Fine craftsmanship

Carefully supervised work. Custom masonry and joining techniques

Integrated arts

Frequent combinations of water, mosaics, glass, sculpture, and perhaps a secondary material

Mottos

Inspirational inscriptions often carved into the chimneypiece to foster good living

Low chimneys

Broad roof openings that joined together all fireplace flues

Top: Wood molding around a brick fireplace remodeled in 1896 and an asymmetrical Usonian hearth. Bottom: A raised customdesigned grate in California and inset glass tiles at the May house.

HOME AND STUDIO

⠿ Good friend, around these hearth-stones speak no evil word of any creature. ⠿
Frank Lloyd Wright
Motto on Home and Studio living room inglenook

The playroom fireplace was topped with a fanciful mural by Orlando Giannini based on a story of the genii and the fisherman. Its far horizon served as another means of dissolving the chimney mass. Roman brick was used quite unconventionally on all the walls of the room, creating an earthy base for the airiness of the barrel-vaulted ceiling.

EACH OF THE SIX FIREPLACES IN Wright's Home and Studio is innovative. The living room fireplace uses roman brick, some of it tapered to create a large semicircular arch. Carved at the top of the oak mantelpiece are the words "Truth Is Life," a variation of his Lloyd Jones family motto, "Truth against the world." Hinged panels permit storage of special objects to be admired in the cozy inglenook. A mirror above the chimneypiece creates the illusion that the fireplace has no flue.

When the dining room was added to the house in 1895, the basket-weave pattern of terra-cotta floor tiles was continued up the chimney wall. Once again, Wright opened the top of the mantelpiece with a recessed shelf to reduce the verticality of the mass.

In his studio library, Wright placed a window over the fireplace—creating a mystery about where the smoke went. But in the drafting room, the arched brick fireplace rises two stories, sharing the chimney with the adjoining office fireplace. There Wright and his apprentices gathered to celebrate new and completed commissions and to discuss their dreams of a new architecture.

EARLY WORK

⊞ It refreshed me to see the fire burning deep in the masonry of the house itself. . . . A real fireplace at the time was extraordinary. ⊞
Frank Lloyd Wright
Kahn Lectures, 1930

For the Oak Park house remodeled for his friend Charles Roberts in 1896, Wright devised a mantel cabinet with an intricate, Sullivanesque fretwork design to illuminate the natural grain of the oak. Angled mirrors within the cabinet created a spatial illusion—a mystery about the solidity of the mass—as they did when placed above other Wright fireplaces of the period.

A REVIEW OF WRIGHT'S EARLY HOUSES shows that he may have been shopping for his own style: experimenting with various techniques for handling the fireplace, not yet accepting its structural mass.

While working for Adler and Sullivan in 1891, Wright designed the city house for the James Charnleys of Chicago. Its fireplace, unlike those of his mature years, was faced with marble and surrounded by richly carved wooden panels as Louis Sullivan, his mentor, would have liked. He often said that wood carving forced the material to do things against its nature, yet he used it here.

By 1896 the brick fireplace of the Heller house, flanked by simple wood panels and delineated with wood molding, had achieved an integrity with the wall and contributed to a strong horizontality. In several of his after-hours "bootleg" designs, Wright placed the fireplace in a corner, mirroring the polygonal bay opposite it. In other early Chicago-area houses—Blossom (1892), Goan (1893), and Winslow (1894)—he used an inglenook, a common feature in Queen Anne houses, to create a spatial change within the rooms so that they were not merely boxes.

P R A I R I E S T Y L E

D R A W N F R O M T H E M I D W E S T . 1 9 0 0 - 1 9 0 9

BY 1900 WRIGHT HAD BEGUN TO use the chimney mass as a vertical element that pinned his houses to the ground. Layers of horizontal forms radiated from this core in various cross-axial plans.

Most of his Prairie Style houses had fireplaces in bedrooms as well as in the living and dining rooms and were like those for the Willitses (1901), the Frickes (1901), the Bartons (1903), the Coonleys (1907), and Mrs. Thomas Gale (1904): simple, straightforward planes or piers of brick, usually roman, surrounding a large rectangular opening that was wider than it was tall. Horizontal counterpoints were provided in each individualized design through artistic use of stone lintels, plinth blocks, wood decks, and wood banding.

Custom hardware continued a house's geometry. Among the earliest were andirons for the Davenport house (1901), their iron spheres strengthening the composition. In the Dana-Thomas house gallery (1902), Springfield, Illinois, Wright used art glass ceiling lights to balance any heaviness. The sides of the yellow brick fireplace were bent like arms to gather everyone together.

⊞ The reality of the house is order. The blessing of the house is contentment. The glory of the house is hospitality. The crown of the house is coolness. ⊞

Motto on Heath house
mantel (1904)

The Robie house fireplace (1906) in Chicago (opposite) was recessed, with the hearth below floor level, and had split flues with an opening between them.

In the Darwin Martin house reception room (1904), Buffalo, New York (pages 26–27), the bold arch with a tapered brick fan was a graceful counterpoint to rectilinear lines.

Integral ornament varied
from a light fixture set into
the Bogk house fireplace
(1916) in Milwaukee (above)
to slivers of iridescent glass in
the horizontal mortar joints
of the May fireplace (1908),
Grand Rapids, Michigan (left).

The Henderson house (1901),
Elmhurst, Illinois (pages 30–31),
has a unique hooded—
almost sculpted—fireplace.

TALIE∫IN

TALIE∫IN, WRIGHT'∫ HILL∫IDE RETREAT near the Wisconsin River, has twenty-three uniquely designed limestone fireplaces scattered around its rambling quarters. Similar in appearance to those in the Welsh farmhouses of his ancestors, the Taliesin fireplaces were used for supplemental heat and were decidedly functional. But each has its own idiosyncratic personality—so much so that each fire had to be built differently. Some needed vertical fires, some fires set deep; others demanded roaring blazes or the aid of grates; some needed a preheated chimney or a simultaneous fire in the adjoining fireplace. Casting their light and warmth into the rooms, fires of all forms were an integral part of life at Taliesin.

Typical of many features there, the fireplace in the living room has survived two major fires and has been reworked at least three times since it was built in 1911. The current composition was completed in the 1950s and features a large saw-cut lintel. The rustic limestone, like the stone for the entire house, was quarried nearby and laid as it was found in horizontal layers, with some stones projecting, the mortar barely visible. Unlike the

⠿ Wright looked at Taliesin as an accretion of time, like a rolling snowball gathering history along the way. ⠿

Robert Burley, 1994

The Chinese statue inset into the irregular stone of Taliesin's guest room fireplace draws the eye upward to the window above. The ceiling in the room has been raised, adding to the overall drama of Wright's composition.

The fireplace in Wright's
Taliesin studio has retained
the rugged masonry of its
original design for eight
decades, while other parts
of the room were repeatedly
redesigned. His mother's
portrait is above the mantel.

⁛ Wright regarded the hearth
as an Indian campfire taken
indoors. ⁛

Donald Hoffmann
Frank Lloyd Wright:
Architecture and Nature, 1986

Prairie Style fireplaces, the Taliesin openings were
slightly more vertical than horizontal and the compositions became more asymmetrical with each redesign.

Two of the fireplaces have fragments of Chinese
art set into the stone, remnants of the 1925 fire. A vertical cranny in the guest room fireplace as it was rebuilt
became the home for a statue of the Chinese goddess
of mercy, Kwan Ying.

Since the garden room was added in the 1950s,
the fireplace in the "pink loggia" has been open on three
sides. Its cantilevered form replaced its earlier, more
rugged, symmetrical design but retained the shards of
blue-and-white Chinese roof tiles salvaged from the fire
and placed in a stone pier. Wright's bedroom was also
enlarged around the same time and its fireplace changed
to its present, more abstract form.

In Wright's studio the fireplace is close to its
original 1911 appearance, the large opening—nearly
four feet square—surrounded by a large hearth. Its
patina of heavy use tells of the many years it warmed
Wright as he called forth his designs.

CALIFORNIA DESIGNS

⠿ Hollyhock house presents a world where . . . the four basic elements of nature, earth, air, fire and water are encountered and nature and architecture are synchronized. ⠿
Hiroshi Murata
Frank Lloyd Wright
Retrospective, 1991

The central fireplace core of the Freeman house (1923) (opposite) allows other walls to be open and airy. The simple forms and geometric textures recall ancient ruins and pre-Columbian temples.

The sculpted mantel is pivotal to the theatrical Hollyhock house fireplace (pages 38–39).

THE FOUR TEXTILE-BLOCK HOUSES that Wright designed for Los Angeles–area clients have fireplaces that seem to be molded from the sandy desert earth. Their cavelike appearance makes them look cool in summer and cozy in winter.

In the Storer house (1923), the fireplace openings are generous. Chimney blocks step back, creating vertical shadows—the solid mass rising proudly. No effort was made to reduce the sense of verticality. Also decidedly vertical, the Ennis fireplace (1923) features a wisteria mosaic overmantel similar to ones Blanche Ostertag and Orlando Giannini executed decades earlier for the Hussers (1899) and Darwin Martins (1904).

Wright's fifth area residence, the Hollyhock house in Hollywood (1917), was designed for Aline Barnsdall. Its fireplace is the central focus of the interior. Built of precast concrete block, it rises like an altar and is rich with symbolism. A gold-tiled pool surrounds the hearth—a cool foil to the fire. Above, diffused light filters through a trellis-covered skylight, illuminating the fireplace and creating an almost spiritual composition.

1930ſ MAſTERPIECEſ

WINGſPREAD AND FALLINGWATER. 1935-37

THE MAJEſTIC, FREEſTANDING, curved brick fireplace core of Wingspread, which Wright designed for the Herbert Johnsons in 1937, opens on each of its four sides. The pinwheel design of this house near Racine, Wisconsin, radiates from its towering, sculptural form. Wright attended to every detail as the masons laid five hundred bricks a day, pressed and raked on a curve.

Of the four fireplaces sharing the same chimney at Fallingwater (1935), the living room design is the grandest. With its sandstone boulders and tumbling waterfall, the wooded site in Mill Run, Pennsylvania, had long been a vacation retreat for Liliane and Edgar J. Kaufmann, who especially liked to bask in the sun on the largest rock. This formation eventually became the center of their new home: the hearth. Rising from the polished flagstone floor, it establishes the rustic feel of the sandstone fireplace composition. All the stone was quarried nearby, cut according to the natural strata in thin slabs and laid with nearly invisible mortar joints. The natural cantilevers of the rock are repeated in both the structural design of Fallingwater and the masonry detailing of its fireplaces.

At Wingspread the vertical joints in the fireplace were tinted red to match the brick, creating horizontal lines as streamlined as the corporate office building Wright also designed for the same client.

Shelves and nooks created by the sculptural stone fireplace in Fallingwater's main bedroom (pages 42–43) became natural homes for the Kaufmanns' art objects and books.

Fallingwater's cast-iron
kettle sphere, suspended over
the living room fire on a
swivel arm, rests in a concave
nest when it is not in use.
Its curves are part of the
minor theme of the house's
primarily rectilinear design.

TALIESIN WEST

SCOTTSDALE, ARIZONA. 1937 - 59

LIKE ALL THE MASONRY WALLS OF Taliesin West, Wright's winter home in the Arizona desert beginning in 1937, the fifteen fireplaces were built of ruble stones. They were set in forms that were then filled with concrete. Variegated colors—from reds and purples to grays and tans—and textures in the building material itself were all the ornament needed for these flat, vertical planes.

Nearly every room required its own fireplace to cut the morning and evening desert chill. Their varied rustic forms rise from the desert floor, born of the same elements. One in the sun cottage is nearly large enough to stand in. Others are so wide they can be used to warm trays of food. Most have canted walls, mirroring the angle of the McDowell Mountains on the horizon.

Just two years before he died in 1959, it is said that Wright carefully selected the stones to be used for the new fireplace in the garden room. Rather than have only flat boulders showing, he customized the design so that several rounded shapes—one with moss still attached—could protrude from the mass.

Unlike those at Taliesin in Wisconsin, fireplace openings at Taliesin West tended to be more horizontal. Because of the nature of the building material, they did not have single lintels spanning the opening but were punctuated by plinth blocks. The large masses presented bold forms similar to prehistoric cyclopean masonry.

▦ No Wright house is without a fireplace, not because of the need for heat but because of those intangible psychological values—warmth, comfort, protection and family unity. ▦

H. Allen Brooks
The Pope-Leighey House, 1969

USONIAN HOUSES

RESIDENCES OF MODEST COST. 1936-59

:: The fireplace is the geometric and symbolic center of the house, for here is where the sacred flame of the family is kept burning. . . . Connecting the vault of heaven with the underworld, the conduit opens into the dwelling of man to warm and sustain him with fire. It is the cosmic center of the house where all the forces of the landscape are concentrated. ::

Thomas Beeby
In *The Nature of Frank Lloyd Wright,* 1988

At the Lovness studio (1955), Stillwater, Minnesota, rustic stone blocks are cantilevered over the opening of the corner fireplace, built by the owners.

CONSTRUCTION OF USONIAN HOUSES, the simplified residences Wright designed after 1936, usually began with a masonry core featuring a large fireplace. It was the functional and structural heart of the house, stabilizing the airiness of the surrounding space. Wall posts or piers and the roof would be added next, followed by the infill of wall panels and glass. Without the fireplace core, Usonian houses might have appeared flimsy.

A fireplace's profile was created from the module used in the house. Its placement depended on the grid incised into the floor. Those on a rectangular or square grid would be right-angled. Those on a hexagonal or triangular grid would have angles of 60 or 120 degrees. Curved forms were used for circular grids. A house's masonry type also contributed to the design of its fireplace. While some used local stone or concrete block, most were constructed of brick in shades of red to brown.

The first Jacobs house (1936), built in Madison, Wisconsin, is also known as Wright's first Usonian. Using standard brick, he created a simple asymmetrical fireplace reflecting the rectangular module. One large plinth block

The parallelogram module of the Anthony house (1949), Benton Harbor, Michigan, gave shape to its asymmetrical fireplace. Built of local limestone, it is a pivot drawing all to the heart of the room.

serves as a shelf while accentuating the third dimension of the mass. The fireplace alcove of another early Usonian, the Goetsch-Winckler house (1939), Okemos, Michigan, uses overlapping L-shaped masonry masses like shapes on the floor plan itself. An L-shaped table fit like a puzzle piece around one end close to the workspace (kitchen).

Wright tried a number of variations in his later Usonians. Marble scraps in various natural shades were used for the masonry of the Neils house (1949) in Minneapolis. Its fireplace of finely cut shards was stationed at the junction of the living and bedroom arms of the plan and reflected the shift in angles. Surrounding the fireplace of the concrete block Brown house (1949), Kalamazoo, Michigan, is a shallow pool—a simpler variation of the technique he used to mix opposing elements in the Hollyhock house. In another concrete block design, the Pearce house (1950), Bradbury, California, Wright combined curves with the house's square module.

The overriding raison d'etre of each of Wright's fireplaces was a place for fire—for the warmth and light and human feelings that radiated from it.

A low pool around the Brown house hearth (right) opposes fire and water.

Opposite, top: Wright placed the fireplace at his Usonian Exhibition house (1953) in New York City on an outside corner. He gave his son David Wright a curved, concrete block design (1950). Bottom: The Zimmerman hearth (1950) is at the home's core. The Neils chimney was cantilevered and outfitted with a suspended, round iron kettle.

Concrete block and mahogany (pages 54–55) converge to create a solid anchor for the airy Pearce house living room.

FRANK LLOYD WRIGHT

Abernathy, Ann. *The Oak Park Home and Studio of Frank Lloyd Wright*. Oak Park, Ill.: Frank Lloyd Wright Home and Studio Foundation, 1988.

Baden-Powell, Charlotte. *Fireplace Design and Construction*. London: Longman Group, 1984.

Bolon, Carol R., Robert S. Nelson, and Linda Seidel, eds. *The Nature of Frank Lloyd Wright*. Chicago: University of Chicago Press, 1988.

Clark, Clifford Edward, Jr. *The American Family Home, 1800–1960*. Chapel Hill: University of North Carolina Press, 1986.

Handlin, David P. *The American Home: Architecture and Society, 1815–1915*. New York: Little, Brown, 1979.

Menocal, Narciso, ed. *Wright Studies*. Carbondale, Ill.: Southern Illinois University Press, 1992.

Pfeiffer, Bruce Brooks, ed. *Frank Lloyd Wright: Collected Writings*. Vols. 1 and 2. New York: Rizzoli, 1992.

——. *Frank Lloyd Wright Monographs*. 12 vols. Tokyo: ADA Edita, 1987–88.

Wright, Gwendolyn. *Moralism and the Model Home*. Chicago: University of Chicago Press, 1980.

ACKNOWLEDGMENTS

The author wishes to thank Robert Burley; Tom Casey; William Dring; Penny Fowler, Frank Lloyd Wright Foundation; Meg Klinkow, Frank Lloyd Wright Home and Studio Foundation Research Center; John Thorpe; John Tilton; Lynda Waggoner, Fallingwater; and especially the generous owners of the houses included here. Special appreciation is due Penny and Pat Fahey and Mary and Lars Lofgren for assistance with new photography.

Illustration Sources:

Richard Bowditch: 6–7

© Judith Bromley: 19 top left, 23, 30–31

Richard Cheek: 41

Pedro E. Guerrero: 1, 8, 33, 34, 53 top left and right, 53 bottom right, back jacket

Balthazar Korab: 19 top right, 50–51, 52

K. C. Kratt: 26–27

Christopher Little: 16–17, 42–43, 44–45, 45

John Marshall, courtesy Jeffrey M. Chusid: 37

© Norman McGrath: 48

Jon Miller © Hedrich-Blessing: 2, 21, 24

Eric Oxendorf: 29

Steelcase Inc., Grand Rapids, Mich.: 19 bottom right, 28–29

Ezra Stoller © Esto: 10–11, 15, 46, 53 bottom left

Tim Street-Porter: 13

© Alex Vertikoff: 38–39

Scot Zimmerman: 19 bottom left, 54–55

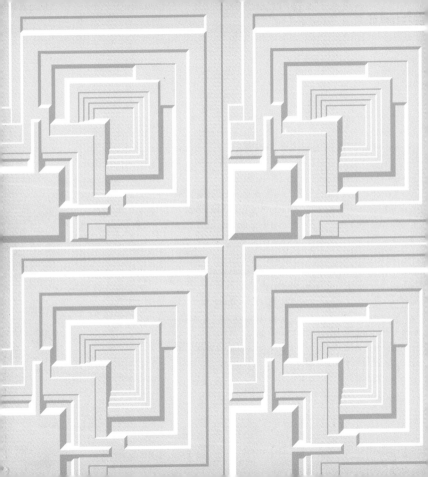